# Tell Me a Story

## Family Folklore

# North American Folklore for Youth

# Tell Me a Story

# Family Folklore

Gus Snedeker

Mason Crest

W

Mason Crest
370 Reed Road
Broomall, Pennsylvania 19008
www.masoncrest.com

Printed and bound in the United States of America.

First printing
9 8 7 6 5 4 3 2 1

Library of Congress Cataloging-in-Publication Data

Snedeker, Gus.
 Tell me a story : family folklore / Gus Snedeker.
    p. cm. — (North American folklore for youth)
 ISBN 978-1-4222-2488-5 (hbk.) — ISBN 978-1-4222-2486-1 (hbk.
series) — ISBN 978-1-4222-9253-2 (ebook)
 1. Families—Folklore—Juvenile literature. 2. Families—History—Juvenile literature. 3. Storytelling—Juvenile literature. I. Title.
 GR465.S64 2013
 398.2—dc23
                        2012011853

Produced by Harding House Publishing Services, Inc.
www.hardinghousepages.com
Cover design by Torque Advertising + Design.

# Contents

# ✳ Introduction

## by Dr. Alan Jabbour

What do a story, a joke, a fiddle tune, a quilt, a dance, a game of jacks, a holiday celebration, and a Halloween costume have in common? Not much, at first glance. But they're all part of the stuff we call "folklore."

The word "folklore" means the ways of thinking and acting that are learned and passed along by ordinary people. Folklore goes from grandparents to parents to children—and on to *their* children. It may be passed along in words, like the urban legend we hear from friends who promise us that it *really* happened to someone they know. Or it may be tunes or dance steps we pick up on the block where we live. It could be the quilt our aunt made. Much of the time we learn folklore without even knowing where or how we learned it.

Folklore is not something that's far away or long ago. It's something we use and enjoy every day! It is often ordinary—

and yet at the same time, it makes life seem very special. Folklore is the culture we share with others in our homes, our neighborhoods, and our places of worship. It helps tell us who we are.

Our first sense of who we are comes from our families. Family folklore—like eating certain meals together or prayers or songs—gives us a sense of belonging. But as we grow older we learn to belong to other groups as well. Maybe your family is Irish. Or maybe you live in a Hispanic neighborhood in New York City. Or you might live in the country in the middle of Iowa. Maybe you're a Catholic—or a Muslim—or you're Jewish. Each one of these groups to which you belong will have it's own folklore. A certain dance step may be African American. A story may have come from Germany. A hymn may be Protestant. A recipe may have been handed down by your Italian grandmother. All this folklore helps the people who belong to a certain group feel connected to each other.

Folklore can make each group special, different from all the others. But at the same time folklore is one of the best ways we can get to know to each other. We can learn about Vietnamese immigrants by eating Vietnamese foods. We can understand newcomers from Somalia by enjoying their music and dance. Stories, songs, and artwork move from group to group. And everyone is the richer!

Folklore isn't something you usually learn in school. Somebody, somewhere, taught you that jump-rope rhyme you know—but you probably can't remember *who* taught you. You definitely didn't learn it in a schoolbook, though! You can study folklore and learn about it—that's what you are doing now in this book!—but folklore normally is something that just gets passed along from person to person.

This series of books explores the many kinds folklore you can find across the North American continent. As you read, you'll learn something about yourself—and you'll learn about your neighbors as well!

# ONE
# What Does Family Mean?

How surprised the mother duck was when the biggest egg in her nest finally hatched. But the creature that emerged from the broken shell looked nothing like the rest of her children.

"Look how big he is!" the mother said to her ducklings. "Much bigger than any of you."

"Ugly, too," one of the ducklings agreed. "Our feathers are yellow, but his are a dull gray."

"He doesn't talk like us, either," quacked another duckling.

The ugly duckling was so mistreated by the others that he ran away. He found a group of wild ducks living on a pond nearby, but when he tried to join them, they said the same things about him.

"You don't look like us!"

"You don't talk like us!"

"Go away!"

They flapped their wings at him and quacked loudly, scaring the ugly little duckling.

He came to a barnyard where a flock of chickens pecked at kernels of corn. "May I eat corn with you?" he asked shyly.

The hen cocked her head and looked him over. "Hmmm, you're a strange looking one. And you talk funny, too."

The ugly duckling knew what was coming, and he left the barnyard before the hen could drive him away.

For a little while, the poor little duckling took shelter in the home of an old lady with a cat. He tried to make friends with the cat. He even tried to act like the cat, since the lady seemed so fond of it. But within just a day or two, the duckling's longing to be in the water overwhelmed him.

"The water?" purred the cat. "You want to go into the water?" He arched his back and gave a loud meow. "You're a strange, strange creature."

At last, tired and sad and longing to find a family of his own, the ugly duckling came to a pond where he saw the most beautiful birds he could imagine. He watched them for an entire day, hiding in the bushes so they wouldn't drive him away. Sometimes the beautiful big birds swam gracefully, their long slender necks reflected in the calm water beneath them. The ugly duckling stretched his neck as far as he could, and felt his own legs ache to swim with them. Sometimes the magnificent birds flew, their powerful white wings sweeping the air and lifting them high above the trees.

The ugly duckling flapped his own wings and, though he tried to be silent, he could not help making one little cry—his own cry that all the other animals had found so strange.

Immediately, the huge birds heard him and answered with cries that sounded just like his. They flew to where he was hiding and landed on the water in front of his bushes. "Come and swim with us!" they said.

The ugly duckling was afraid to join them at first. "I can't. I'm just an ugly duckling."

The big birds said, "No, you are one of us!"

The duckling couldn't believe it, but when they finally coaxed him into the water, he caught sight of his own reflection. He was no longer gray. His feathers were white now, like theirs. His neck had grown as long and as graceful as theirs. He spread

his wings with delight and saw that they looked as powerful as the wings of these beautiful birds.

"You are one of us," cried the swans, and he swam away with them, overjoyed to find his real family at last.

Lots of folktales like this one tell about finding your own family. People all want to belong somewhere, just like the ugly duckling. They all want a family

But what is a family anyway? All families have something in common: they share a history, a present, and hopes for the future.

A family tradition can be something as simple as eating a meal together.

Most people's families are related to them. They live with their mom and/or dad, their siblings, and maybe their grandparents or cousins.

That doesn't have to be true. Maybe you live with your mom and stepdad. Or you were adopted. Or you live in a foster home. Even people who aren't related to you can be your family.

Families share **traditions** and **customs**. The celebrate holidays in special ways. They tell certain jokes that only they understand. That's all part of a family's **folklore**, a way of learning things that belongs just to them.

Think of it this way: members of a family are *inside*. Everyone else is *outside*. There's some sort of boundary between who's in a family and who isn't.

---

## FAMILY TRADITIONS

Some family traditions can be as simple as sitting down together for the evening meal. Or they can be as complicated as dressing in special clothes to celebrate a holiday. All families choose to perform traditions differently. Most family experts agree that even the little things that you enjoy over and over again within your family have a big impact on you.

How would you describe your family's traditions for the following events?

- visiting with relatives
- family reunions
- family fun (activities like biking, bowling, picnics, etc.)
- mealtimes
- birthdays

Here are some other things that a family is (or should be), according to an author named Edith Schaeffer:

- a group of people who spend time together all the time, and who help each other
- the first place where people have relationships

## FIGHTS AND FOLKLORE

Families don't always get along. Every family has its problems at some point. Each family deals with its problems differently. Some families fight and then never talk about the argument again. They "sweep it under the rug." Other families talk about why they are fighting. They try to fix the problem by talking about it.

In some cases, family fights are just too hard to fix. Parents get divorced. Or kids run away. Maybe you get mad at your cousins and stop talking to them. Maybe a great-aunt no longer speaks to your other great-aunt. She hasn't for 20 years. These things can become part of the family folklore.

It's always best, though, to try to fix the problems before they become too big. But sometimes it just isn't possible. Then you have to accept them and move on.

- a safe place during hard times
- a way to learn
- a museum for memories

Family folklore includes folk customs that have to do especially with the family. Folklore involves stories and songs. It includes traditions, foods, and jokes. When a family shares folklore, it feels more like a family.

Older members of the family pass on folklore to kids. Your grandma could tell you a poem that she always says when she walks down the sidewalk. Your uncle might have a favorite story that he tells at every birthday gathering.

Both of these things help to bind your family closer together. They pass down things **unique** to your family. They tell you, "This is *your* family."

# ✳ TWO
# Older and Younger

**Words to Understand**

*Superstitions* are beliefs that say something supernatural is the reason why something happens. For instance, a black cat causes bad luck. That's a superstition. There's no real reason to believe it that is based on science.

*Generations* are all the people born at about the same time. Your grandparents are one generation, your parents and aunts and uncles are another generation, and you, your brothers and sisters, and your cousins are another.

We learn a lot from our parents and grandparents. When we're little, everything is new. Somebody has to teach us!

Your family is a good place for teaching and learning. Your family members teach you about good behavior and bad behavior. They teach you about nature. They teach you about why things work the way they do. This is all part of your family's folklore.

Families can use **superstitions** or sayings to teach. Maybe you've heard "Step on a crack, break your mother's back."

One family says this poem:

*Grasshopper, grasshopper, grasshopper gray,*
*Grasshopper, grasshopper, get out of my way.*

The family has its own special story behind the poem. When Grandma was five years old, she had to walk miles to get to school. The large, gray grasshoppers on the road would freeze her in her tracks. She didn't want to step on them! Then she made up a rhyme to get them to move—and sometimes they would.

Years later, she told the story to her daughter. Then her daughter told it to a third generation. See how stories are passed on?

Stories and poems aren't the only way to pass on family history. There are also pictures, videos, and recordings.

You can watch family videos of when your cousins were little. You can watch your mom graduate high school. You can look at old photographs and see exactly what your grandpa looked like when he was in the army.

Families are also a big way we learn about religion. Parents' ideas about God and religion shape what their kids believe.

Our parents bring us to temple, or the mosque, or church (or not). Our later ideas about religion probably come from what we learn when we are young.

Families sometimes teach about religion in a formal way. They take their kids to church. They make them go to religious classes.

## FOOD AS A LINK TO THE PAST

Some families are linked by special recipes or ways of eating. They're passed down through the generations. Some of these are everyday foods. Others are for the special dishes prepared for holidays or celebrations.

One family has parents that were raised during the Great Depression (a time in the United States when many people were very poor, back in the 1930s). This family still sometimes eat the foods that were available during that hard time. These foods include mashed potato sandwiches for lunch, and cracker soup for breakfast. Mashed potato sandwiches are pretty obvious (just put mashed potatoes between two slices of bread). For those who need help with cracker soup, here is the recipe:

Place saltine crackers in a cereal bowl. Pour hot coffee over the crackers, add a little whole milk and lots of sugar. (Enjoy *quickly*, before the crackers turn totally to mush.)

Maybe this sounds gross to you. But for the family that grew up with it, it sounds delicious!

Other families pass down other sorts of recipes. Maybe your Jewish grandmother makes noodle kugel. She's famous in your family for it. Your mother knows how to make it too. Sometimes she makes it at home. She told you that someday she'll teach you how to make the kugel too.

But families also teach about religion through folklore. Here's an example of a poem that one mother taught to her son to say when he was scared:

*Dear God, such fright!*
*Don't let Satan bite.*
*Keep me safe, I pray,*
*To live another day.*

He may pass this little poem on to his children. And it will become a piece of family folklore.

A family might tell a story about the miracle that saved Dad from certain death. He had lung cancer, but God saved him. The older **generations** in the family are teaching the younger ones that God is a real and loving force for them.

Family religious folklore can include objects too. For example, a Jewish family cherished a prayer shawl that was passed down from father to son. Great-Grandpa brought it from Europe when he moved to America. He passed it on to his son. Then his son passed it on to his son. And so on.

## CHRISTIAN FAMILY STORIES

Christianity in particular has a lot of stories about family. Here's the story of the Prodigal Son from the Christian Bible. It uses a story about family to help teach a lesson about the way God loves us.

A man had two sons. The younger son told his father, "I want my share of your estate now before you die." So his father agreed to divide his wealth between his sons.

A few days later this younger son packed all his belongings and moved to a distant land, and there he wasted all his money in wild living. About the time his money ran out, a great famine swept over the land, and he began to starve. He persuaded a local farmer to hire him, and the man sent him into his fields to feed the pigs. The young man became so hungry that even the pods he was feeding the pigs looked good to him. But no one gave him anything.

When he finally came to his senses, he said to himself, "At home even the hired servants have food enough to spare, and here I am dying of hunger! I will go home to my father and say, 'Father, I have sinned against both heaven and you, and I am no longer worthy of being called your son. Please take me on as a hired servant.'"

So he returned home to his father. And while he was still a long way off, his father saw him coming. Filled with love and compassion, he ran to his son, embraced him, and kissed him. His son said to him, "Father, I have sinned against both heaven and you, and I am no longer worthy of being called your son."

But his father said to the servants, "Quick! Bring the finest robe in the house and put it on him. Get a ring for his finger and sandals for his feet. And kill the calf we have been fattening. We must celebrate with a feast, for this son of mine was dead and has now returned to life. He was lost, but now he is found." So the party began.

*(Luke 15:8–24, New Living Translation)*

# THREE
# Who Are You?

It's a big world out there. It can be hard to figure out how you fit into it. Fortunately, our families can help us out. Family folklore helps shape how we think of ourselves. It gives us an *identity*.

We always belong to our families. The first relationships you have are with whomever takes care of you when you're little. That could be your mom and/or dad. Or your grandparents. Or your aunt and uncle.

**Your family is the place where you learn many important things. Things like how to ride a bike . . . how to pray . . . how to treat others.**

One way that you know you belong to a family is that you share a past. You share some of the same experiences. Then you can use those experiences to figure out who you are.

One family is proud that they are kind to animals. All the kids know that Great-Grandpa never killed spiders. He picked

## FAMILY IDENTITY

Kids who don't have a family or family folklore sometimes have a hard time. Without family, it's hard to figure out who we are when we're little.

For example, the U.S. government used to separate Native American kids from their parents. They wanted to make them less native. So they sent them to schools to teach them to be more American. It was a terrible experience for these families. Parents complained that when their children returned home, they were strangers. They had lost their family identities.

Other Native American children were sometimes placed in foster families. One woman with a foster family said: "Please help me find out who I am. My mother was Indian, but we were taken from her and put in foster homes. They wouldn't tell us anything, not even a story. . . . I don't remember now who I am."

## DEFINING FAMILY MEMBERS

A single episode can represent the whole personality of one relative. For example, not many family members even remember Great Uncle Otto. But the whole family knows who he is. He's the one who worked in the bank the day it got robbed. He helped get the police by slipping out a side door. He was a hero! What else did Uncle Otto do during his lifetime? Nobody knows.

Sometimes, family folklore can be wrong or hurtful. Dad might be known as a jolly joker, when really his humor sometimes makes people feel bad. Aunt Melissa may be known as the family's shy old maid. In truth, she's really an intelligent and competent woman.

them up in his hand and brought them outside. Now everybody in the family does this. They all know that they care about spiders and other creatures. It's part of who they are.

Another family tells the story about how Grandma lived in a war camp in North Africa. It was a really hard life. But she survived because of her strength.

Everyone else in the family tries to copy Grandma. If she could survive that, then they can work through tough times too.

Both of these stories tell family members, "You are not alone." Your family shares the same **values** as you do.

Sometimes it's just nice to know that you know the same stories as everyone else in your family. They don't really teach anything. But you, your brother, your cousins, your parents, aunts and uncles, and grandparents all have heard the same story thousands of times. When you hear it, you know you're part of a family.

One family tells the story of Aunt Ellie. When she was little, she disappeared. Her parents thought she had drowned or had been kidnapped. They looked and looked. Finally, they found her stuck in the **outhouse**!

Family folklore also has to do with how families look or act. Lots of people in your family might look alike. You have the same nose. Or you're all short. Or you all have freckles.

Family stories often poke fun at how everyone in a family acts. The Clingmans refuse to talk to each other before they have coffee in the morning. There are lots of jokes about that. Everyone knows that they're a Clingman because they're so grumpy when they wake up.

Every family has stories like these. If you think about it, you'll probably realize you know some family stories too.

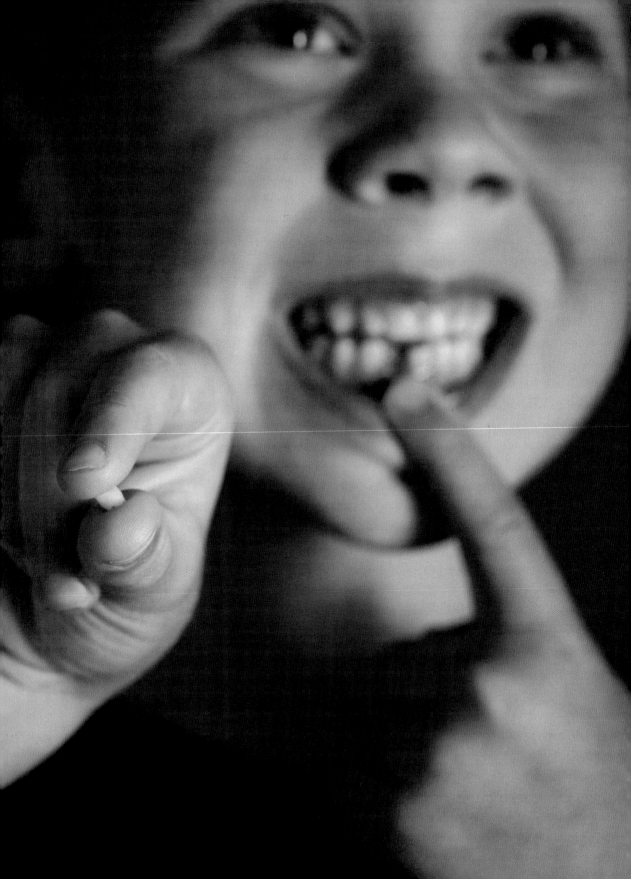

# FOUR
# Celebration!

**Words to Understand**

*Ceremonies* are formal sets of acts that are always done the same way to celebrate some important occasion.

*Milestones* are events that mark an important stage in a person's life. For example, going to kindergarten is a milestone. So is learning to drive. Getting your first job is another. The word comes from an old custom of placing stones beside the road to mark how far travelers had gone.

One way that families stay close is by celebrating. They do certain things to mark special occasions. Those special occasions are a part of their very own folklore. The occasions can be just about anything.

## Lost Teeth

When you lose a tooth, do you put it under your pillow? The tooth fairy comes in the night, takes the tooth, and leaves money. This is a common tradition in lots of families.

Each family does it a little differently. In some families, the tooth fairy leaves a little note. Some kids use a special cup or envelope for the tooth. Traditions about losing teeth are fun for both kids and the adults in the family!

## Birthdays

Birthdays are a big cause for celebration in most families. Many American families have the same sorts of birthday traditions.

The birthday person often gets to choose what to do for the whole day. If you want to go to the zoo, that's what happens. If you want a big birthday party, your family puts one together.

There are special foods for birthdays. Most families make or buy a birthday cake for the birthday person. There are candles in it, usually one for each year. Everyone sings "Happy Birthday." Then the birthday girl or boy blows all the candles out and makes a wish. He or she opens up presents and cards. This probably seems pretty familiar.

But each family usually adds on their own extra traditions. Are there extra verses to "Happy Birthday" at your parties? Do your parents give you special presents? Are there special foods?

The most special birthdays are the ones that mark *milestone* years. For Jewish boys and girls, 13 is a special year. They have bar and bat mitzvahs. These are special *ceremonies* that mean the children are now considered adults in their religion.

For a lot of Americans, 16 is a special year. Girls especially have "Sweet Sixteen" birthday parties. For Mexican girls, 15 is more important. That's when they celebrate their *quinceñera*.

## Thanksgiving

Just about everybody in the United States celebrates Thanksgiving. Most families do some things the same way. They make a big meal. The whole family gets together. Somebody watches the Macy's Thanksgiving Day parade or football on TV.

A Thanksgiving meal celebration.

But each family has its own customs. Instead of turkey, maybe your family serves lasagna or another dish. Your mom makes recipes from the Philippines, where she was born. There's always ice cream for dessert.

Thanksgiving can also be a time to tell family stories. Everybody is all together. That's the best time to pass down family folklore.

## Christmas

Christmas is another holiday that can be unique in every family. Some celebrate the religious side of Christmas. They go to church or bake a birthday cake for Jesus.

Other families don't focus on religion at all. It's more of a time for family and for celebrating winter.

In some families, Christmas dinner is the big meal. In others, it's Christmas Eve dinner. Each family makes different foods.

Then there are the totally unique traditions. For example, one family has the annual "burying Aunt Lillian." After all the presents are opened, the children in the family gather up the ripped wrapping paper in great crackling armfuls. The 70-year-old Aunt Lillian gets down on the floor. And then the kids all cover her with every scrap of paper they can find. The paper shifts, just slightly, and one pale, bony finger extends upward. This is the signal for more shrieks and more wildly tossed paper.

This family has a tradition of wearing crowns as part of their holiday celebration.

Eventually the adults take pity on Aunt Lillian and gather up the wrapping paper.

## Weddings

Weddings are another time everyone in the family comes together. Every wedding is a little different, but they share some traditions in common.

Brides usually wear white. The couple exchanges rings. People bang on glasses at dinner so that the couple kisses. All of these things are old customs. Each family has a slightly different take on them.

Wedding traditions from India are very different from wedding customs that came from Europe. For example, the bride usually wears red instead of white!

People of lots of different nationalities live in the United States. Weddings might look a little different depending on where the people getting married originally came from. For example, at some Indian and Pakistani weddings, women get their hands pained in an orange-red design called mehndi. The bride has especially detailed designs.

## A HANUKAH TRADITION

The dreidel is a wooden top used to celebrate the Jewish holiday of Hanukah. No one seems exactly sure why. Throughout Jewish history, some rulers have forbidden Jews to study the Torah (the Jewish religious book), or to practice their religion. It is thought that sometimes when Jews were studying the Torah, they kept a dreidel at hand so that if soldiers appeared they could pretend to be playing with one of the tops. The dreidel could also have come from a spinning top the Germans had as far back as the Middle Ages. Symbols are put on the sides of the dreidel, and a game is played that depends on the symbol that comes up when the top is spun. It's a good game for children and families!

Going through old family photographs together can be a rewarding way to learn about your family's past.

# ✳ FIVE
# The Never-Ending Chain

Families do a lot. They are the place where kids learn. They provide support and help for people. They give people a sense of identity.

Family folklore is one of the most important ways that people can feel like part of a family. When you share memories, customs, and stories with other members of your family, you know you belong.

Family folklore is like a chain that connects you to the past. One day it will connect you to the future too, to the next generation. This chain stretches back long before your memory or even your grandparents' memories—and it reaches into the future. It's a way of passing on parts of your very own identity to the generations that will come next.

This just happens. It's the way families and folklore work, without anyone doing anything out of the ordinary. But sometimes families like to collect their folklore. They make scrapbooks or family recipe books.

Think about collecting your own family's folklore. Collect things that are unique to your family. They could be stories. Or jokes. Or special words that only your family uses.

Try interviewing older members of your family. They might have family stories you've never heard before. The authors of a book called *A Celebration of Family Folklore* have a few suggestions if you want to do this:

1. Start with a question that you know has an answer. Ask about a family story you've already heard.
2. Don't ask questions that are too general. Be very specific. Don't say, "Tell me about your childhood." Whoever you're interviewing won't know where to start! Instead, ask, "How old were you when you got your first car?" or something like that.
3. Don't ask questions that can be answered with just a yes or a no. You want long answers and stories.
4. Don't ask about things the person isn't comfortable talking about. If your grandpa fought in a war, he might not want to talk about it. That's okay.

5. Don't worry if the person starts telling you something that doesn't answer your question. It could be an interesting story anyway.

6. Use props. You can start conversations using old letters or pictures. They can trigger memories and stories.

7. Be sensitive. If your relative is old, he or she might get tired of answering after awhile.

8. Try to give everyone in your family a chance to answer your questions.

Now put it all together. Write down a family history. Make a scrapbook. Or a movie. That way, your whole family can share in what you've learned. Here are some good questions to get you started:

- Where does your last name come from?
- When did your family come to the United States? Where did they come from?
- How did your parents and grandparents meet?
- What are your family's favorite recipes?
- Does your family have any important *heirlooms*?
- Why did the people in your family pick their jobs?

You can help make a link to the never-ending chain of family folklore!

# Find Out More

## In Books

Anthony, Louis. *Family Folklore*. New York: Author House, 2008.

Drake, Jane. *My Family and Me: A Memory Scrapbook for Kids.* Toronto: Kids Can Press, 2002.

————. *My Grandfather and Me: A Memory Scrapbook for Kids.* Toronto: Kids Can Press, 1999.

————. *My Grandmother and Me: A Memory Scrapbook for Kids.* Toronto: Kids Can Press, 1999.

Enochs, J. B. *Little Man's Family.* Kiva Publications, 2009.

Stone, Elizabeth. *Black Sheep and Kissing Cousins: How Our Family Stories Shape Us.* Walnut, Calif.: Transaction Publishers, 2004.

## On the Internet

**Family Folklore:**
**How to Collect Your Own Family Folklore**
www.smithsonianeducation.org/migrations/seek2/family.html

**Family History Scrapbooks:**
**How to Scrapbook Your Family History**
genealogy.about.com/cs/scrapbooks/a/family_history.htm

# Index

# Picture Credits

# About the Author and the Consultant

Gus Snedeker is proud of his heritage as a Dutch American. He loves to study the stories and traditions of the various groups of people who helped build America. He has also written several other books in this series.

Dr. Alan Jabbour is a folklorist who served as the founding director of the American Folklife Center at the Library of Congress from 1976 to 1999. Previously, he began the grant-giving program in folk arts at the National Endowment for the Arts (1974-76). A native of Jacksonville, Florida, he was trained at the University of Miami (B.A.) and Duke University (M.A., Ph.D.). A violinist from childhood on, he documented old-time fiddling in the Upper South in the 1960s and 1970s. A specialist in instrumental folk music, he is known as a fiddler himself, an art he acquired directly from elderly fiddlers in North Carolina, Virginia, and West Virginia. He has taught folklore and folk music at UCLA and the University of Maryland and has published widely in the field.